——— NATASHA D. VARNEY ———

Berlin

CHRISTMAS MARKETS 2023-2024

Your Ultimate Festive Guide To Experience The Joy Of
The Season At The City's Xmas Markets

BERLIN

CHRISTMAS MARKETS 2023

Your Ultimate Festive Guide To Experience The Joy Of The Season At The City's Xmas Markets

Natasha D. Varney

TABLE OF CONTENTS

Map Of Berlin

INTRODUCTION

In the heart of Berlin, a city rich in history, I stumbled upon a hidden secret. It was a chilly evening, and I found myself walking through brightly lit streets. Little did I know that this night held the key to an amazing discovery.

As I strolled through the city's streets, I felt like I was getting closer to something extraordinary. The streets were filled with stories of celebration, and the air smelled like warmth and excitement. It was a special evening when Berlin's soul transformed into something truly magical.

Berlin's Christmas markets, ancient traditions, had come to life in the city. The Brandenburg Gate was covered in twinkling lights, and it felt like the city was about to reveal a long-kept secret. I was lucky to be a part of it.

During this adventure, I realized that Berlin's Christmas markets were more than just annual events. They were a gateway to a world where traditions, flavors, and stories blended beautifully. It was a place where history and the present came together, and where you could feel the city's heartbeat under the starry sky.

This book is your key to the city's hidden treasure, an invitation to explore Berlin's holiday magic. Here, you'll uncover stories etched into the city's very stones, savor flavors passed down through generations, and immerse yourself in the music and joy that warms the coldest nights.

But this isn't just a guidebook; it's a journey to create your own Berlin Christmas market experience. With insider tips and personal touches, you'll make this journey uniquely yours.

So, dear traveler, as I reveal this enchanting tale, I invite you to join me on an adventure that will captivate your senses, lift your spirits, and uncover a world of magic that's been hiding in plain sight. The adventure begins here, and the story is yours to write.

CHAPTER 1

Brief History of Berlin Christmas Markets

The history of Berlin Christmas markets dates back centuries. The earliest known Christmas market in Berlin was held in 1530 on the Molkenmarkt. This market was originally intended to provide a place for people to buy food and supplies for the Christmas holiday. However, it quickly became a popular gathering place for people to socialize and enjoy the festive atmosphere.

Over the years, Christmas markets became increasingly popular in Berlin. By the early 19th century, there were dozens of Christmas markets held throughout the city. These markets were typically held in public squares and featured stalls selling food, drinks, and gifts.

In the early 20th century, Berlin Christmas markets began to attract visitors from all over the world. The city's reputation for having some of the best Christmas markets in the world grew even further after World War II.

Today, Berlin is home to over 100 Christmas markets. These markets are held from late November to early January and attract millions of visitors each year. The most popular Berlin Christmas markets include the Gendarmenmarkt Christmas Market, the Alexanderplatz Christmas Market, and the Potsdamer Platz Christmas Market.

Berlin Christmas markets offer a variety of activities and attractions for visitors of all ages.

Visitors can browse stalls selling traditional German Christmas decorations, gifts, and food and drinks. They can also enjoy live music and performances, ice skating, and other winter activities.

Berlin also has several unique and hidden gem Christmas markets. These markets offer a more alternative and offbeat experience. For example, the RAW-Gelände Christmas Market is held on a former railway repair complex and has a more industrial and alternative vibe. The Weihnachtsmarkt am Schlesischen Tor Christmas Market is held in a park along the Spree River and offers stunning views of the city skyline.

No matter what your interests are, you are sure to find a Berlin Christmas market that you will love. These festive gatherings offer a unique and unforgettable experience for visitors of all ages.

What to Expect at a Berlin Christmas Market?

Festive Atmosphere: Berlin Christmas markets are known for their festive atmosphere. With twinkling lights, festive music, and the delicious aromas of roasted chestnuts and gingerbread wafting through the air, it's hard not to get into the Christmas spirit.

Beautiful Decorations: Each market is adorned with unique and eye-catching decorations. Expect to see intricate ornaments, magnificent Christmas trees, and creative light displays.

Handcrafted Gifts: The markets are a treasure trove of handcrafted gifts. You'll find items like wooden toys, delicate glass ornaments, handmade candles, and more. These make perfect gifts or souvenirs for loved ones.

Food and drink: Berlin Christmas markets offer a wide variety of traditional German food and drinks, including Glühwein (mulled wine), Bratwurst (grilled sausage), Kartoffelpuffer (potato pancakes), and Lebkuchen (gingerbread cookies). You can also find international food options at many of the markets.

Live Entertainment: Most markets feature live entertainment. You can enjoy traditional holiday music, carolers, and even theatrical performances. The festive sounds and sights will add to the holiday spirit.

Kids' Activities: Many Berlin Christmas markets offer activities for kids of all ages, such as ice skating, carousel rides, and face painting. There are also often Santa Claus grottos where kids can meet Santa and receive a small gift.

Cozy Nooks: Seek out the cozy nooks and corners where you can sit around open fires or heaters. These spots are perfect for warming up while enjoying your snacks and drinks.

Shopping Opportunities: In addition to gifts, you can also shop for winter clothing, decorations for your home, and other seasonal items.

Tradition and Unity: The most heartwarming aspect of Berlin's Christmas markets is the sense of tradition and unity they bring. Locals and visitors alike come together to celebrate the holiday season in a spirit of togetherness.

Winter activities: Many Christmas markets offer winter activities such as ice skating, ice slides, and carousel rides.

CHAPTER 2: PLANNING YOUR TRIP

Best Time To Visit?

Choosing the best time to visit Berlin's Christmas Markets depends on your preferences, but there are a few factors to consider. Here are some recommendations on the best times to visit:

Early December: The first half of December is an excellent time to visit if you prefer smaller crowds and a more relaxed atmosphere. Markets are fully operational, and you can enjoy the festive spirit without the peak-season rush.

Weekdays: If you can, visit the markets on weekdays. They tend to be less crowded compared to weekends, allowing for a more leisurely experience.

Before December 24th: The Christmas Markets typically run until December 24th, so visiting before this date ensures you can experience the full holiday atmosphere and enjoy the markets at their busiest.

Evening Visits: To fully appreciate the magical ambiance, consider visiting the markets in the evening. The beautifully illuminated stalls and decorations come to life after sunset.

After Christmas: Some markets continue to operate after Christmas, offering a chance to enjoy the holiday atmosphere even into the post-Christmas period.

Tips for Planning Your Visit

1. Choose the Right Market: Berlin boasts a variety of Christmas markets, each with its unique charm. Research and pick the one that suits your preferences, whether you're looking for a historic market, a family-friendly atmosphere, or a specific theme.

2. Check the Dates: Christmas markets typically open from late November to December 31st. Make sure to check the specific dates for the market you plan to visit, as they can vary.

3. Dress Warmly: Berlin winters can be quite cold, so don't forget to bundle up. Bring a warm coat, gloves, a scarf, and comfortable shoes for walking.

4. Plan Your Timing: The markets are busiest in the evenings and on weekends. To avoid crowds, consider visiting during weekdays and in the early afternoon.

5. Bring Cash: While many stalls accept cards, it's a good idea to carry some cash, especially for smaller purchases and food stalls.

6. Try the Local Food: Don't miss the opportunity to taste traditional German and Berliner holiday treats like bratwurst, potato pancakes, and roasted nuts. And, of course, sample the famous mulled wine, Glühwein.

7. Shop for Unique Gifts: Berlin's Christmas markets are excellent places to find one-of-a-kind gifts. Explore the handcrafted items and support local artisans.

8. Enjoy the Entertainment: Take time to watch the live performances, listen to carolers, and immerse yourself in the festive atmosphere.

Plan your transportation: Berlin has a great public transportation system, so it's easy to get to the Christmas markets by train, bus, or tram. However, the markets can get crowded, so it's best to avoid peak travel times.

9. Keep an Eye on Opening Hours: Check the opening and closing times of the market you plan to visit, as they may vary from one market to another.

10. Be Mindful of Security: Berlin is a safe city, but it's always a good idea to keep an eye on your belongings, especially in crowded areas.

11. Consider Guided Tours: If you want to learn more about the history and culture of the markets, consider joining a guided tour. It can provide you with valuable insights and make your visit even more memorable.

How To Get There??

❖ By Plane

Berlin is a major international travel destination, and there are many direct flights to Berlin from all over the world. The main airport in Berlin is Berlin Brandenburg Airport (BER), which is located about 25 kilometers (16 miles) from the city center. There are also two smaller airports in Berlin: Berlin-Tegel Airport (TXL) and Berlin-Schönefeld Airport (SXF).

To get from the airport to the city center, you can take the S-Bahn, the U-Bahn, or a taxi. The S-Bahn is a fast and efficient train system that connects the airport to several points in the city center. The U-Bahn is a slower but more affordable option.

❖ By car

Driving to Berlin from another European city is also a viable option, but it is important to factor in the time and cost of parking. Parking in Berlin can be expensive, and it may be difficult to find parking near the Christmas markets. If you do decide to drive to Berlin, be sure to book your parking in advance.

❖ By Train

Berlin is well-connected to the European rail network, and there are many direct trains to Berlin from major cities in Europe. The main train station in Berlin is Berlin Hauptbahnhof (Berlin Central Station), which is located in the city center.

To get from the train station to the Christmas markets, you can take the U-Bahn, the S-Bahn, or a bus. The U-Bahn is the best option for reaching most of the Christmas markets. The S-Bahn is a good option for reaching the markets in the western part of the city. Buses are also a good option, but they can be slower than the U-Bahn and S-Bahn.

How To Get Around The Christmas Markets??

Public Transportation: Berlin has an extensive public transportation network, including the U-Bahn (underground train), S-Bahn (suburban train), and buses. The U-Bahn and S-Bahn are the fastest and most efficient ways to get around, and there are stops near most of the Christmas markets. Buses can be a good option if you are looking for a more scenic route.

Taxis: Taxis are also readily available in Berlin, and they can be a convenient way to get around, especially if you are traveling with a group of people or have luggage. However, taxis can be expensive, so they are not always the most economical option.

Biking: Berlin is a bike-friendly city, and there are many bike paths throughout the city. Renting a bike is a great way to get around the Christmas markets, as it is a quick and easy way to get from one market to another.

Walking: Walking is a great way to get around the Christmas markets, as they are all located within a relatively small area. This is also a good way to soak up the atmosphere and take in the sights and sounds of the markets.

Best Hotels For Berlin Christmas Markets??

❖ Hotel de Rome

If you prefer a 5-star hotel with a historical touch, Hotel de Rome is housed in a beautifully restored bank building. It's centrally located, making it easy to access Christmas Markets like Alexanderplatz and Potsdamer Platz.

HOTEL DETAILS

Address: *Behrenstraße 37, 10117 Berlin*

No of Rooms: *145 Rooms*

Price Range: *From €853 per night*

Contact Line: *+49 30 4606090*

❖ Adina Apartment Hotel Berlin Hackescher Markt

If you are seeking a more spacious and comfortable option, Adina Apartment Hotel offers well-equipped apartments with kitchen facilities. It's located near the Hackescher Markt, where you'll find a charming Christmas Market.

HOTEL DETAILS

Address: An d. Spandauer Brücke 11, 10178 Berlin

No of Rooms: 145 Rooms

Price Range: From €220 per night

Contact Line: +49 30 2096980

❖ Hotel Adlon Kempinski Berlin

This iconic 5-star hotel is located near Brandenburg Gate and is known for its luxury and exceptional service. During the Christmas season, it's beautifully decorated, and you'll have easy access to many of Berlin's Christmas Markets.

HOTEL DETAILS

Address: Unter den Linden 77, 10117 Berlin

No of Rooms: 385 Rooms

Price Range: From €320 per night

Contact Line: +49 30 22610

❖ Leonardo Hotel Berlin Mitte

This is a great mid-range option for travelers who want comfort without breaking the bank. It's close to many Christmas Markets, including the one at Brandenburg Gate.

HOTEL DETAILS

Address: Bertolt-Brecht-Platz 4, 10117 Berlin

No of Rooms: 309 Rooms

Price Range: From €79 per night

Contact Line: +49 30 374405000

❖ Generator Berlin Prenzlauer Berg

If you're a budget traveler, Generator Hostel is a trendy and social place to stay. It's located in

Prenzlauer Berg, and while it may not be as upscale, it provides a cozy base for exploring Christmas Markets in that area.

HOTEL DETAILS

Address:

Storkower-Strasse-160-Berlin-10407

No of Rooms: *238 Rooms*

Price Range: *From €15 per night*

Contact Line: *+49030408189000*

❖ Hotel Oderberger

Located in the lively Prenzlauer Berg neighborhood, Hotel Oderberger is a historic hotel that combines a rich past with modern comfort. The hotel exudes grandeur and history, providing a premium experience for travelers who appreciate luxury and proximity to Berlin's Christmas Markets.

HOTEL DETAILS

Address: Oderberger Str. 57, 10435 Berlin

No of Rooms: 70 Rooms

Price Range: From €122 per night

Contact Line: +49 30 780089760

❖ Hotel Indigo

Ideally located in the heart of East Berlin, Hotel Indigo provides a contemporary and welcoming atmosphere. With a range of modern and well-designed rooms, this hotel offers a stylish and comfortable base for exploring Berlin's Christmas Markets, catering to mid-range budgets.

HOTEL DETAILS

Address: Mühlenstraße 13-19, 10243 Berlin

No of Rooms: 118 Rooms

Price Range: From €172 per night

Contact Line: +49 30 29772060

❖ Hotel Amano East Side

Hotel Amano East Side is positioned at the junction of the Friedrichshain and Kreuzberg neighborhoods, offering easy access to the East Side Gallery and a vibrant array of eateries and bars. With a modern and vibrant atmosphere, this hotel provides mid-range pricing, striking a balance between style and affordability in the heart of Berlin.

HOTEL DETAILS

Address: Stralauer Pl. 30-31, 10243 Berlin

No of Rooms: 174 Rooms

Price Range: From €53 per night

Contact Line: +49 30 29772060

CHAPTER 3: EXPLORING BERLIN CHRISTMAS MARKETS

❖ Gendarmenmarkt Christmas Market

The WeihnachtsZauber Gendarmenmarkt in Berlin is the most popular and visited Christmas market, surrounded by the Concert Hall, German and French Churches, and Checkpoint Charlie. The market features a gigantic Christmas tree, live choir performances, and a stage with a live choir. The wooden stalls offer unique handmade products, gourmet treats, and hot beverages. The WeihnachtsZauberBar offers fine wines. The market ends on New Year's Eve with a DJ party and a large fireworks display, making it a popular destination for gifts and souvenirs. The market is a must-visit if you want an unforgettable festive experience.

INFORMATION:

- *Address:* Gendarmenmarkt 2, 10117 Berlin
- *DATE: Date: From 27th, November – 31st, December 2023*

- *Opening/Closing Hours: Sunday to Thursday (12 pm to 10 pm), Friday and Saturday (12 pm to 11 pm),* **Christmas Eve** *(12 pm to 6 pm),* **New Year's Eve** *(12 pm to 1 am)*

- *Admission: €2 Entry fee,* **FREE** *entry for children (under 12), and Monday to*

*Friday from (12 am - 2 pm) **FREE** entry for all (except on 24th/25th/26th and December 31st of December)*

- *Contact Line: +49 (0)30 – 20 91 26 32*

How To Get There

Bebelplatz is situated between the State Opera, the Law Faculty of Humboldt University, and the Hotel de Rome. Paid parking is available in the following multi-story car parks: CONTIPARK underground car park Friedrichstadt-Passagen, VINCI Park Friedrichstraße, and APCOA Parking Leipzigerstraße.

I suggest that you use public transportation.

S-Bahn: S1, S2, S3, S5, S7, S9, S25, S26, S75
Friedrichstraße, S1, S2, S25, S26 Potsdamer
Platz
U2 Hausvogteiplatz, U5 Museumsinsel or
Stadtmitte, U6 Französische Str.
Bus: 100, 300 Staatsoper

❖ Charlottenburg Palace Christmas market

If you love palaces, the Charlottenburg Palace
Christmas Market is a must-visit. Located in the
shadow of a gorgeous 18th-century Baroque
palace, this market is a fairy tale come true.

The spectacular backdrop of the palace is lit up
with changing colored lights, creating a romantic
atmosphere. It's the perfect spot to have a cup of
warm Glühwein with your loved ones.

The market also offers a winter open-air restaurant, a petting zoo, free nostalgia carousels, and over 250 local and international exhibitors offering culinary treats and unique crafts.

Be sure to visit Charlottenburg Palace itself, the former private residence of Sophie Charlotte, the first Queen consort in Prussia.

INFORMATION:

- *Address:* Spandauer Damm 22-24, 14059 Berlin

- *DATE: From 27th, November — 31st, December 2023*

- *Opening/Closing Hours: Monday to Thursday (2 pm to 10 pm), Friday to Sunday (12 pm to 10 pm),* **Boxing Day**

(12 pm to 8 pm), **Christmas Eve** *(Closed)*

- *Admission:* Free

How To Get There

The Christmas market is located on Spandauer Damm in Berlin-Charlottenburg, just in front of Charlottenburg Palace.

Because there are just a few parking places available, using public transportation is the best option.

S-Bahn (underground train) lines: S41, S42, and S46 Westend

U-Bahn (underground train): U2 Sophie-Charlotte-Platz

Bus: 109, M45 Luisenplatz/Schloss Charlottenburg, and 309 Klausenerplatze

❖ Spandau Christmas market

The Spandau Old Town Christmas Market is the largest in Berlin, with over 250 stalls during the week and over 400 on weekends. Thousands of twinkling lights create a festive and joyful atmosphere, centered around a large fir tree and a nativity scene with live animals.

Wednesdays are family days, with the opportunity to take a photo with Santa Claus. Every Friday evening, a rock concert begins at 6:00 p.m.

Although Spandau is a suburb on the city's outskirts, it is easily accessible from Alexanderplatz or Zoologischer Garten by S-Bahn.

INFORMATION:

- *Address:* *Kammerstraße 6, 13597 Berlin*

- *DATE:* *From 27th November - 23rd December, 2023*

- *Opening/Closing Hours: Sunday to Thursday (11 am to 8 pm), Friday & Saturday (11 am to 10 pm)*

- *Admission: Free*

Tips For Visiting

A visit on Wednesday is particularly advantageous for families since not only does Santa Claus come to visit, but there are also special deals for children and families.

Combine your visit with a stroll around Spandau's old town and some shops. For a shopping spree, the Spandau Arcaden shopping center is also close. Look for the cannonball from the Napoleonic conquest embedded in the outside wall of the Gothic church of St Nikolai at Reformationsplatz.

A visit to the Spandau citadel, with its exhibitions and the Juliusturm tower, is particularly attractive to the whole family.

How To Get There

U7 Altstadt Spandau U-Bahn (underground train)

Berlin-Spandau S-Bahn (overground train) S3, S9

The Christmas market is easily reached by taking the U-Bahn line U7. Exit at Altstadt Spandau station. Berlin-Spandau is also well connected by long-distance, regional, and S-Bahn stations. The journey takes about 20 minutes from the S-Bahn station Zoologischer Garten in City West.

❖ Berliner Weihnachtszeit at the Rotes Rathaus

The Berliner Weihnachtszeit at the Rotes Rathaus is one of the most popular and festive

Christmas markets in Berlin. Held annually from November to December, the market attracts millions of visitors from all over the world.

The market is located on the square in front of the Rotes Rathaus (Red City Hall), the seat of the Berlin Senate. The iconic building provides a stunning backdrop for the market, which is decorated with thousands of twinkling lights and festive decorations.

Visitors to the Berliner Weihnachtszeit can enjoy a variety of Christmas-themed activities and attractions, including:

Shopping: The market features over 100 stalls selling a wide variety of Christmas goods, including traditional German Christmas ornaments, handmade gifts, delicious food, and drinks. Visitors can find everything they need to get into the holiday spirit!

Ice skating: The market features a large outdoor ice rink, where visitors of all ages can enjoy skating around the Christmas tree.

Entertainment: The Berliner Weihnachtszeit offers a variety of entertainment options, including live music, dance performances, and children's activities. There is always something to see and do at the market!

One of the highlights of the Berliner Weihnachtszeit is the Christmas pyramid, which is decorated with over 5,000 lights and stands as the largest walk-in Christmas pyramid in Europe. On the ground floor of the pyramid, visitors can enjoy snacks and refreshments, while the platform on top offers stunning views of the city.

Another popular attraction at the Berliner Weihnachtszeit is the Christmas forest, where visitors can wander through a magical wonderland of fir trees and twinkling lights. There is also a petting zoo with donkeys, sheep, and ponies, as well as a Santa Claus grotto where children can meet Santa and have their photos taken.

INFORMATION:

- *Address: Spandauer Straße, 10178 Berlin*

- *DATE: From 27th November - 7th January 2024*

- *Opening/Closing Hours: Monday to Friday (12 p.m. to 10 p.m.), Saturday & Sunday (11 a.m. to 10 p.m.),* **Christmas Eve** *(Closed),* **New Year's Eve** *(Open till 8 p.m.),* **Boxing Day** *(11 a.m. to 9 p.m)*

- *Admission: Free*

Tips For Visiting

Take a ride on the panoramic Ferris wheel and enjoy the views of Unter den Linden, the Brandenburg Gate, and Potsdamer Platz.

Wait eagerly for Santa Claus with your children: He flies his sleigh across the sky every day at 4:30, 6:30, and 8:30 p.m. You could also have souvenir pictures with Santa Claus at the photo booth located beside the big Christmas tree.

How To Get There

The Christmas Market is located in Berlin-Mitte at the foot of the television tower, between the Rotes Rathaus and St. Marienkriche.

S-Bahn (overground train) lines: S3, S5, S7, S9, and S75 Alexanderplatz

U-Bahn (underground train): U2, U5, U8 Alexanderplatz

M4, M5, M6, M10 Tram Spandauer Straße/Marienkirche

Bus lines: 100, 200, M4, M48, TXL Spandauer Straße/Marienkirche, 248, M48 Berliner Rathaus

❖ Kaiser Wilhelm Memorial Church Christmas Market

The Kaiser Wilhelm Memorial Church Christmas Market is set against the backdrop of the iconic church and is a short walk from the Berlin Zoo. The market's 25-foot Christmas tree and festively decorated stalls will put you in the holiday spirit.

Over 170 wooden stalls offer handmade tree ornaments, toys, and other unique gifts and souvenirs. I bought a lovely angel-shaped Christmas ornament from one of the stalls.

On New Year's Eve, the market hosts a fireworks display at 6:00 PM, 8:00 PM, 10:00 PM, and midnight.

INFORMATION:

- *Address:* Breitscheidplatz 1, 10789 Berlin

- *DATE:* From 27th November - 7th January 2024

- *Opening/Closing Hours:* Sunday to Thursday *(11 am to 9 pm), Friday & Saturday (11 am to 10 pm),* **Christmas Eve** *(11 am to 2 pm),* **Christmas Day** *(1 pm to 9 pm),* **New Year's Eve** *(11 am to 8 p.m.),* **New year Day** *(1 pm to 9 p.m)*

- *Admission:* Free

Tips For Visiting

The Kaiser Wilhelm Memorial Church's Christmas market is one of the few that remains open after Christmas. So you can start your New Year at the Advent market. You can support the German Red Cross's homeless projects by purchasing a delicious mulled wine from their stall.

Take a look at the West Berlin landmark, the Memorial Church, while visiting the Christmas market.

After that, soak in the city's Christmas atmosphere with a stroll along Kurfürstendamm, which has the world's longest Christmas lighting area, or do some last-minute Christmas shopping at the Bikini Berlin or the Europacenter department stores.

How To Get There

I recommend traveling by public transportation. The Europacenter multi-story car park is available.

S-Bahn (suburban rail) S3, S5, S7, and S9 Zoological Garden

U-Bahn (underground train) Zoologischer Garten, U2, U9 Kurfürstendamm U1

Buses: M45, M46, M49, X9, X10, X34, 100, 109, 110, 200, 204, 245, 249, Zoological Garden

❖ Lucia Christmas Market

The Lucia Christmas Market, held annually at the Kulturbrauerei in Prenzlauer Berg, is widely considered to be the most beautiful Christmas market in Berlin. The historic clinker brick buildings provide a perfect backdrop for this Nordic celebration, which features charming red and white wooden cottages selling traditional handicrafts, classic Christmas market snacks, and typical Scandinavian delicacies such as moose goulash, reindeer salami, elk meatballs, salmon potato soup, and Finnish waffles. Of course, the Lucia Christmas Market also offers traditional German Christmas fare such as bratwurst and crêpes. But be sure to try the Nordic mulled wines, which are available in over 20 different varieties, including Swedish Glögg, Finnish Glögi, and Icelandic Jolaglögg.

INFORMATION:

- *Address:* Schönhauser Allee 36, 10435 Berlin

- *DATE:* From 27th November - 22nd December 2023

- *Opening/Closing Hours:* Monday to Friday (3 pm to 10 pm), Saturday & Sunday (1 pm to 10 pm)

- *Admission:* Free

Tips For Visiting

Families will enjoy visiting the Lucia Christmas Market during the afternoon hours when the atmosphere is more tranquil. After dark, the market is transformed into a romantic oasis with thousands of twinkling lights, making it a perfect place for couples to stroll hand-in-hand.

Nordic culture enthusiasts should not miss Saint Lucy's Day on December 13th, a celebration of Swedish folklore.

The Kulturbrauerei complex, where the market is held, also houses clubs, restaurants, and a cinema, so you can easily extend your evening out. The museum in the Kulturbrauerei offers a fascinating permanent exhibition and rotating special exhibitions on various aspects of everyday life in the GDR, all with free admission.

A winter walk through the festively decorated neighborhood and across the tranquil Kollwitzplatz is another beautiful experience.

How To Get There

Visitors arriving by car will find an underground parking lot on Sredzkistraße, which is often crowded. Therefore, it is it is advisable to use public transport.

U-Bahn U2 Eberswalder Straße or Senefelderplatz Tram 12, M1, and M10 Eberswalder Straße

Schönhauser Allee S-Bahn (overground train) S8, S41, S42, S85

❖ Alexanderplatz Christmas Market

The Alexanderplatz Christmas Market is one of the largest and most popular Christmas markets in Berlin. With over 100 stalls selling traditional crafts, Christmas decorations, jewelry, and other trinkets, as well as the delicious aromas of bratwurst, gingerbread, and mulled wine wafting through the air, it is a truly festive experience.

One of the highlights of the market is the Christmas pyramid, decorated with over 5,000 lights and standing as the largest walk-in Christmas pyramid in Europe. On the ground floor of the pyramid, visitors can enjoy snacks and refreshments, while the platform on top offers stunning views of the city.

The Christmas Market also offers a variety of entertainment for all ages. There are daily show programs, fairground rides for children, a Ferris wheel, and an ice rink. There is also a party venue resembling a traditional wooden hut, where adult visitors can enjoy a drink and dance well into the night.

Whether you are looking for unique gifts, delicious food and drinks, or family-friendly entertainment, the Alexanderplatz Christmas Market is the perfect place to get into the holiday spirit.

INFORMATION:

- *Address:* *Alexanderplatz, 10178 Berlin*

- *DATE:* *From 27th November - 26th December 2023*

- *Opening/Closing Hours:* *Monday to Sunday,(10 am to 10 pm)* **Christmas Eve** *(10 am to 4 pm)*

- *Admission:* *Free*

Tips For Visiting

You and your children can do a few relaxing loops or curling on the ice rink in the middle of the square. Come inside the warm interior of the covered Santa Claus party house and have a wonderful time.

Combine your Christmas market walk with a visit to Museum Island's museums. Alternatively, take advantage of the central location by doing some last-minute Christmas shopping at nearby shops or the Alexa shopping center.

How To Get There

I recommend you travel by public transport.

S-Bahn (overground train) S3, S5, S7, S9 Alexanderplatz S+U

U-Bahn (underground train) S+U Alexanderplatz U5, U8

BUS M48, 100 Alexanderplatz/Memhardstraße

TRAM M2, M4, M5, M6 U Alexanderplatz/Memhardstraße

❖ Christmas market in the Späth'schen Baumschulen

The Christmas market in the Späth'schen Baumschulen (Späth's Tree Nursery) is a unique and charming Christmas market located in the Treptow-Köpenick district of Berlin.

The market is set in the historic tree nursery, which is over 200 years old. The market stalls are located in the nursery's greenhouses and open-air spaces, creating a festive and atmospheric setting.

Visitors to the Christmas market can enjoy a variety of activities, including:

1. Browsing the stalls for unique Christmas gifts, including handmade crafts, traditional German Christmas ornaments, and delicious food and drinks.
2. Enjoying live music and dance performances.
3. Taking a horse-drawn carriage ride through the festively decorated nursery.
4. Visiting the Christmas crib and Santa Claus grotto.

INFORMATION:

- *Address:* Späthstraße 80/81, 12437 Berlin

- *DATE:* on the first **three Advent weekends** 2023 (2nd/3rd December,

9th/10th December and 16th/17th December 2023)

- *Opening/Closing Hours:* *Monday to Sunday,(11 am to 8 pm)* **Christmas Eve** *(10 am to 4 pm)*

- *Admission:* *€8, for children up to 16 years (free of charge), reduced admission of €5 for students, pupils, and trainees up to 28 years of age, and guests with a severely disabled pass.*

Tips For Visiting

Buy your Christmas tree here. There is a wide range of trees available, including Nordmann firs, pines, and red spruces. You may also choose between dwarf pines and dwarf spruces with root balls for permanent placement in tubs on your terrace, or large Nordmann firs for transplanting into the garden.

The Christmas markets have entrances on Ligusterweg, Späthstraße, and Königsheideweg.

How To Get To There

The Späth'schen Baumschulen is situated in the southeast Berlin borough of Treptow-Köpenick. If you arrive by car, you'll see a large car park on Ligusterweg.

I recommend traveling by public transport.

Bus lines: 170 and 265 run along Baumschulenstr./Königsheideweg.

❖ LGBTQIA Winterdays and Christmas Avenue

The LGBTQIA Winter Days and Christmas Avenue is a festive Christmas market held annually at Nollendorfplatz, the heart of Berlin's LGBTQIA community. The market features a variety of attractions, including:

Stalls selling traditional German Christmas food and drinks, as well as unique LGBTQIA-themed gifts.

Live music and DJ sets from LGBTQIA artists.

A "party hut" where visitors can dance and celebrate the holiday season.

INFORMATION:

- *Address:* *Nollendorfplatz, 10777 Berlin*

- *DATE: From 10th November - 23rd December 2023, Winterdays (10th to 25th November, Christmas)*

- *Opening/Closing Hours: Monday to Thursday,(4 pm to 10 pm), Friday to Sunday (3 pm to 10 pm)*

- *Admission: Free*

Tips For Visiting

In 10 minutes, you can stroll from Nollendorfplatz to the Schwules Museum or go on a Christmas shopping spree along the Ku'damm. If you're looking for that special present to put beneath the Christmas tree, the boutique stores on Fuggerstraße are sure to have it.

How To Get To There:

The LGBTQIA Winter Days at Nollendorfplatz are well served by public transportation. I recommend you leave the car at home.

U1, U2, U3, and U4 Nollendorfplatz

M19, 106, 187, N2, N26 Nollendorfplatz bus lines

❖ Nordische Märchenweihnacht at Schloss Britz

The Nordische Märchenweihnacht (Nordic Fairy Tale Christmas) at Schloss Britz is hosted annually at Schloss Britz, a historic manor house located in the Neukölln district of Berlin. The market is transformed into a winter wonderland, with twinkling lights, festive decorations, and snow-covered trees. Visitors can stroll through the market and enjoy the enchanting atmosphere, while also browsing the stalls for unique Christmas gifts, delicious food and drinks, and handcrafted goods.

One of the highlights of the Nordische Märchenweihnacht is the Nordic-themed entertainment program. Visitors can enjoy live music and dance performances, as well as traditional Nordic storytelling and storytelling for children.

INFORMATION:

- *Address:* Alt-Britz 73, 12359 Berlin

- *DATE:* on the first **three Advent weekends** 2023 (1st to 3rd December, 8th to 10th December and 15th to 17th December 2023)

- *Opening/Closing Hours:* Friday (2 pm to 9 pm), Saturday & Sunday (11 pm to 9 pm)

- *Admission:* adults €3, children €2, free entry up to 6 years

Tips For Visiting

Combine your stay at Schloss Britz during Nordische Märchenweihnacht with a visit to the Museum Neukölln or a look at the famous Hufeisensiedlung housing estate, which was built in 1925 in the style of Berlin Modernism.

How To Get There:

The Nordische Märchenweihnacht at Schloss Britz is located in Neukölln's Britz district. I recommend using public transportation since parking options are limited.

U-Bahn (underground train): U7 Parchimer Allee
Bus: 181, M44 Britzer Damm/Mohriner Allee, and M44, M46 Fulhamer Allee.

❖ Historical Christmas Market on the RAW grounds

The Historical Christmas Market on the RAW grounds in Berlin is a unique and enchanting Christmas market experience. Set in a former railway depot, the market is transformed into a medieval village with torches, jugglers, and acrobats creating an immersive atmosphere.

Visitors can browse the stalls for traditional German Christmas handicrafts, medieval delicacies, and hot mead. Children can enjoy the Ferris wheel, wooden carousel, troll forest, archery, and crossbow shooting.

INFORMATION:

- *Address: Revaler Straße 99, 10245 Berlin*

- *DATE: 16th November to 22nd December 2023)*

- *Opening/Closing Hours: Monday to Friday (3 pm to 10 pm) Saturday & Sunday (12 pm to 10 pm)*

- *Admission: Monday to Wednesday (free), Thursday to Sunday (€2), children from 6-16 years & those in historical costumes (€1), for children under 6 years admission is free of charge.*

How To Get There

The RAW Cultural Center in Friedrichshain hosts a Christmas market. RAW is an acronym that stands for Reichsbahnausbesserungswerk (Reichsbahn repair station). Take public transport. The RAW grounds are easily accessible by S-Bahn and U-Bahn, as well as by tram or bus.

S-Bahn (subway): S3, S5, S7, S75, S9 Warschauer Straße

U-Bahn (overground train): U1, U3 Warschauer Straße

Bus: Helsingforser Platz, 347 Berlin, 248 S Warschauer Straße is a street in Berlin.

Tram: M10, M13 S Warschauer Straße

❖ Winter magic in Advent at Wendenschloss Lido

The Winter Magic in Advent at Wendenschloss Lido is hosted annually from December to January at the Wendenschloss Lido, a popular swimming spot located in the Treptow-Köpenick district of Berlin.

The market is set in the lido's grounds, which are transformed into a winter wonderland with twinkling lights, festive decorations, and snow-covered trees. Visitors can stroll through the market and enjoy the enchanting atmosphere, while also browsing the stalls for unique Christmas gifts, delicious food and drinks, and handcrafted goods.

Things You Can do:

- Visit the Christmas market stalls: The market features a variety of stalls selling traditional German Christmas food and drinks, as well as unique gifts and handicrafts. Visitors can find everything from Glühwein (mulled wine) and bratwurst to handmade jewelry and Christmas ornaments.
- Go ice skating: The Lido's ice rink is open during the Winter Magic in Advent

market and is a great place to enjoy a winter activity with family and friends.

- Take a ride on the Ferris wheel: The Ferris wheel offers stunning views of the market and the surrounding area.

INFORMATION:

- *Address:* Möllhausenufer 30, 12557 Berlin

- *DATE:* all four Advent weekends in December 2023

- *Opening/Closing Hours:* Winter magic (from noon), brunch (from 10 a.m. to 2 p.m.), Christmas dinner by reservation (from 6 p.m.)

- *Admission: free, for brunch, dinner, raft rides & other activities*
- *Contact Line: 030 - 84 51 89 07*

How To Get There:

Strandbad Wendenschloss can be reached in about one hour by car or public transport from Alexanderplatz. I recommend using public transport; use the S-Bahn to Köpenick and then change to tram line 62. Walk one kilometer from Wendenschloss station to the lido.

❖ Advent Lichter Genuss at Natur-Park Schöneberger Südgelände

Located in a former railway depot in the Tempelhof-Schöneberg district of Berlin, The Advent Lichter Genuss Christmas market at Natur-Park Schöneberger Südgelände is transformed into a winter wonderland for the holiday season.

Upon arrival at the market, visitors are instantly captivated by the twinkling lights and festive decorations adorning the park's historic buildings and grounds. The air is infused with the sweet scents of Glühwein, bratwurst, and gingerbread, while the sounds of live music and children's laughter fill the air.

One of the things that sets the Advent Lichter Genuss market apart from other Christmas markets in Berlin is its focus on sustainability and social responsibility. The market organizers are committed to reducing the event's environmental impact, and they work with local businesses and organizations to source food, drinks, and crafts.

INFORMATION:

- *Address:* *Rückwärtiger Ausgang S-Bahnhof Priesterweg, 10829 Berlin*

- *DATE: The first two Advent weekends in December 2023 (2nd/3rd and 9th/10th December)*

- *Opening/Closing Hours: Saturday (3 pm to 7 pm), Sunday (12 pm to 6 pm)*

- _Admission:_ *€1 (from 14years), **Annual pass holder** (free admission)*

Tips For Visiting

After visiting the Christmas market, take a stroll around the festive winter nature park and enjoy the enchanting landscape. If there is snow, you may go tobogganing on the Insulaner hill's nearby toboggan run. At the Wilhelm Foerster Observatory, look up into the sky.

How To Get There:

S-Bahn station Priesterweg S2, S25 BUS M76, X76, 170, 246 Priesterweg stop

There is also a park-and-ride car park at the Priesterweg S-Bahn station.

❖ Advent market at the Domäne Dahlem

The Advent Market at Domäne Dahlem is a charming and unique Christmas market held on the grounds of a working organic farm in Berlin. The market is centered around a former manor house from the 16th century, and the old house and adjoining outbuildings form a beautiful backdrop for the festive stalls and activities.

Fun for Young and Old

Domäne Dahlem is not only an open-air museum but also a working organic farm, so visitors can expect to see live animals and smell the nearby wintery fields. This creates a cozy and authentic countryside market atmosphere, making the Advent Market at Domäne Dahlem a perfect place for a family outing.

Children will be delighted by the many activities on offer, including candle-making, ornament decorating, and interacting with live animals. Adults can browse the stalls for high-quality handmade gifts, pottery, and felt products, or simply savor the festive atmosphere while enjoying traditional German Christmas food and drinks.

Traditional Food and Unique Gifts

From around lunchtime, the market bustle is accompanied by live music shows, adding to the magical ambiance. The offerings at the Christmas market include a variety of traditional German Christmas food and drinks, such as goose drumsticks, mulled wine, waffles, and non-alcoholic punch for children.

INFORMATION:

- *Address:* Königin-Luise Straße 49, 14195 Berlin

- *DATE:* The first three Advent weekends in December 2023 (2nd/3rd, 9th/10th and 16th/17th December)

- *Opening/Closing Hours:* Each day (11 am to 7 pm),

- *Admission:* €3.50, reduced: €2 (students, trainees, Berlin Pass holders or severely disabled persons), free admission (children up to 12 years)

Tips For Visiting

Come along with your children, many hands-on activities are waiting for them! Enjoy the rural flair by riding in a bullock cart or horse-drawn carriage. Buy your organic Christmas tree from certified local suppliers here. From 2:00 pm to 6:00 pm you can visit the Domäne Dahlem Museum and hear tales about the cultural history of food. You can also witness artisans at work in the farm's workshops.

How To Get There:

The Domäne Dahlem is situated in Berlin's south-west district of Steglitz-Zehlendorf, next to the Botanical Garden.

There is visitor parking available. U-Bahn (underground train): U3 Dahlem-Dorf

Bus lines: 110 Domäne Dahlem, M11, N3, and X83 Dahlem-Dorf

❖ Alt-Rixdorf Christmas Market

The nostalgic Christmas market at Richardplatz in the heart of Neukölln is a unique and charming experience. Open for one weekend only, the market transforms the old market square into a winter wonderland with paraffin lamps and other historic elements.

Over 200 vendors sell carefully curated Christmas decorations, foods, and more. Handmade toys, tree decorations, and dipped candles are just a few of the unique items available. Visitors can also find honey, homemade jams, brushes, greeting cards, bratwurst, candied apples, cotton candy, mulled wine, hot chocolate, and mead at the stands.

The Rixdorf Christmas market also features a variety of other attractions, including pony riding, a visit of the Three Wise Men with their camels, a historic smithy, and a display of historic carriages.

The Christmas market is a charitable event, with proceeds benefiting neighborhood initiatives in Neukölln.

INFORMATION:

- *Address: Richardplatz 1, 12055 Berlin*

- *DATE: 8th to 10th December 2023*

- *Opening/Closing Hours:* Friday (5 pm to 9 pm), Saturday (2 pm to 9 pm), Sunday (2 pm to 8 pm)

- *Admission:* free

Tips For Visiting

Visit the almost 400-year-old smithy and take home a handcrafted horseshoe as a lucky charm. Do you want to try special delicacies? The Alt-Rixdorf Christmas Market is known to have the tastiest mulled wine in town, so you've come to the right place.

Make plans to take your children to the Christmas market. Children's activities such as visits to Santa Claus or the Christmas witch, as well as pony rides, will make their eyes light up.

If you have time, combine your visit to the Alt-Rixdorf Christmas Market with a visit to the Bohemian Village Museum.

How To Get There:

Richardplatz is situated in the heart of Neukölln's Richardkiez neighborhood. I recommend using public transport for your vacation.

S-Bahn (overground train): S41, S42, S45, S46, and S47 Neukölln
U7 Karl-Marx-Straße
U-Bahn (underground train): U7 Karl-Marx-Straße
Bus: 171, M41, N7 Hertzbergplatz

❖ Weihnachtsrummel on Landsberger Allee

The Christmas carnival on Landsberger Allee is the oldest Christmas market with fairground rides in East Berlin, following the popular Wintertraum Alexa. The tradition began in the 1920s at Berlin Cathedral, with various rides. Showmen later set up stalls at Jannowitzbrücke, Schlossplatz, and Platz der Vereinten Nationen. The market began at the Lustgarten in Mitte with a wooden carousel and rollercoaster and has since moved to Landsberger Allee.

From afar, you can see the twinkling lights of the Winterzauber rides, beckoning you to a world of festive fun and excitement. This Christmas market and funfair on Landsberger Allee is a must-visit for visitors of all ages, with something to offer everyone.

With over 20,000 square meters of space, Winterzauber is home to a wide variety of festive attractions and stalls. From classic Christmas market offerings like mulled wine and gingerbread to thrilling rides and games, there is something for everyone to enjoy.

INFORMATION:

- *Address: Landsberger Allee 300, 13055 Berlin*

- *DATE: 3rd November to 30th December 2023*

- *Opening/Closing Hours: Monday (2 pm to 9:30 pm), Friday & Saturday (1 pm to 11 pm), Sunday & public holidays (12 pm to 9 pm)*

- *Admission: free*

How To Get There:

I recommend traveling by public transport.

Trams: 16, 27, M17, M6, M8 to Arendsweg

bus: 256, N56 to Liebenwalder Str./Landsberger Allee

❖ Winter World and Christmas Market at Potsdamer Platz

Potsdamer Platz's Winterwelt is a popular winter attraction in Berlin, offering a unique blend of festive fun and sporting activities. Unlike traditional Christmas markets, Winterwelt features a thrilling 12-meter-high, 70-meter-long winter slide with views of the Brandenburg Gate. The slide's colorful disco lights are sure to make children's eyes light up, and there are several nearby huts where young and old athletes can refuel with bratwurst, roasted almonds, mulled wine, crêpes, and other treats.

For those who prefer a more relaxed atmosphere, the illuminated lime trees of Alte Potsdamer Straße offer a charming setting for a crafts market and numerous stalls selling Christmas snacks and gifts. Last-minute shoppers can find handmade gifts, Christmas decorations, and children's toys at the market.

INFORMATION:

- *Address:* *Potsdamer Platz, 10785 Berlin*

- *DATE:* ***Winter World****: 28th October to 1st January 2023,* ***Christmas Market:*** *27th November to 26 December 2023*

- *Opening/Closing Hours:* ***Winter World****: (11 am to 10 pm), 24th December (11 am to 2 pm), 19th & 26th November (closed),* ***Christmas***

Market: (10 am to 10 pm), 24th December (10 am to 4 pm)

- *Admission: free (to the Christmas market) €2.5 (toboggan run)*

Tips For Visiting

The Christmas market in Potsdamer Platz is perfect for a family outing, thanks to its sporty winter activities. On weekends, live music and DJs provide a winter party atmosphere for all adult Christmas market visitors. You can continue your tour around the Christmas market with a trip to the shopping center, which is situated directly by the Potsdamer Arkaden and the Mall of Berlin. You'll surely discover some last-minute Christmas presents here.

How To Get There:

I recommend traveling by public transport.

There are parking spaces available at the Potsdamer Platz Arkaden underground car park or in the Parkhaus Sony Center APCOA.

S-Bahn (overground train) stations: S1, S2, S25, S26 S+U Potsdamer Platz

Bus stations: 200, M41, M48, M85, N2 S+U Potsdamer Platz

CHAPTER 4: EVENTS/CONCERTS IN BERLIN DURING CHRISTMAS

December Events In Berlin

❖ Christmas Garden Berlin

Inspired by Christmas at Kew in England, the Christmas Garden in Berlin invites visitors to a magical stroll through the Berlin Botanical Garden. For nearly eight weeks, over a million lights, colorful illuminations, and Christmas-themed 3D figures illuminate the grounds.

Guests of all ages can linger and enjoy the festive illuminations while savoring regional dishes at the Almhütten restaurant. Other highlights include 3D figures of Rudolph and his friends, an enchanted forest, a Singing Tree to hum along to, and magical floating stars in black light. Some interactive installations have been designed specially for selfies. Sound designer Burkhard Fincke will once again provide the perfect soundtrack for the event this year.

INFORMATION:

- *Address:* *Königin-Luise-Straße 6, 14195 Berlin*

- *DATE:* *From 17th November 2023 to 14th January 2024*

- *Opening/Closing Hours:* *Sunday to Thursday (4:30 pm to 9:30 pm), Friday and Saturday (4:30 pm to 10 pm)*

Closed on: 1. 20th, 21st, 27th and 28th November 2023

2. 24th and 31st December 2023

- *Admission: From €16.50*

❖ Christmas at the Tierpark

Christmas in the Tierpark is Berlin's second large-scale light installation, after the Christmas Garden in the Botanical Garden.

During the holidays, you can enjoy a two-kilometer circular walking tour around the colorfully lighted park, where you will be welcomed by 30 light sculptures. Illuminated treetops, shining stars, and light shows on the water lead the way to the festively illuminated Friedrichsfelde Palace. The Christmas experience is rounded off with a "poetic fire garden" and a variety of culinary delights.

INFORMATION:

- *Address:* *Elfriede-Tygör-Straße 6, 10319 Berlin*

- *DATE: From 15th November 2023 to 14th January 2024*

- *Opening/Closing Hours: Sunday to Thursday (5 pm to 9 pm), Friday and Saturday (5 pm to 10 pm), Between 21st December & 7th of January (5 pm to 10 pm)*
  Closed on: 1. 20th, 21st, 27th and 28th November 2023
  2. 24th and 31st December 2023

- _**Admission:** From €15.50_

❖ Baroque Days at the Berlin State Opera

The Baroque Days festival at the Berlin State Opera is dedicated to reviving the original sound of 18th-century opera. This year's festival will feature a triple performance of Medea, with operas by Marc-Antoine Charpentier, Luigi Cherubini, and Georg Anton Benda. The program also includes the children's opera Theseus' Journey to the Underworld and Mozart's Mitridate, Re di Ponto.

The Baroque Days festival is a unique opportunity to experience 18th-century opera in a historically accurate setting. The Berlin State

Opera is one of the most prestigious opera houses in the world, and its productions are known for their high quality and attention to detail.

INFORMATION:

- *Address:* Unter den Linden 7, 10117 Berlin

- *DATE:* From 17th November 2023 to 26th November 2023

- *Admission: Different fees depending on the concert*

❖ Berlin New Year's Eve Run

The market Teufelsberg Race in the Grunewald Forest offers runners of all ages and fitness levels a challenging and scenic course. The

10-kilometer race leads over two hills, Teufelsberg and Drachenfliegerberg, while the 6-kilometer route passes Teufelsberg. Runners can also choose to run the 2- or 4-kilometer race. The race is known for its festive atmosphere, and many runners participate in costume. All finishers are rewarded with celebratory pancakes.

INFORMATION:

- *Address:* *Waldschulallee 43, 14055 Berlin*

- *DATE: 31st December 2023*

- *Start And Finish: Parking lot on Harbigstraße/Waldschulallee (opposite Mommsen Stadium)*

- *Start Time: Between noon & 1 pm*

- *Distances: 10.6, 6.7, 4.4 and 2.4 kilometers*

- *Admission: Between €10 & €28*

• Louis Lewandowski Festival

The Louis Lewandowski Festival is an annual music festival organized by the Association of Friends and Sponsors of the Synagogal Ensemble Berlin. The ensemble is the only one in the world that performs Lewandowski's liturgy every Friday evening, Shabbat morning, and Jewish holiday.

During the festival, the Synagogal Ensemble is joined by other ensembles and choirs from around the world to perform compositions by Lewandowski and other Jewish composers.

INFORMATION:

- *Address: Pariser Platz, 10557 Berlin*

- *DATE: From 14th December 2023 to 17th December 2023*

- *Admission: Different fees depending on the concert*

Film Festivals

❖ Around The World In 14 Films

Around The World In 14 Films is an independent international film festival that showcases 14 extraordinary films from 14 different regions of the world each year. The festival brings these films to Berlin's discerning cinema public, offering a glimpse into the diverse cinematic landscapes of South America, Africa, Europe, the Near East, the Middle East, Central Asia, the Far East, and North and Central America.

Each of the 14 films is presented by a leading German director, actor, artist, or journalist, who introduces the film and the director (if present) and moderates a post-screening discussion with the audience and director.

INFORMATION:

- *Address: Schönhauser Allee 36, 10435 Berlin*

- *Location: Cinema at KulturBrauerei*

- *DATE:* From 1st December to 9th December 2023

❖ Black International Cinema

Black International Cinema Berlin, a festival originating from the Black Cultural Festival, is a cultural event that showcases the contributions of Black people to world culture through film, theater, dance, music, workshops, and seminars. It is produced and directed by Fountainhead® Tanz Théâtre annually in Berlin and other European and US-American cities. The festival focuses on artistic, cultural, or political works that align with the educational, social, artistic, and economic interests of people from Africa, the African Diaspora, and those interested in intercultural communication. It is open to all filmmakers and contributes to better understanding and cooperation between people from various cultural, ethnic, national, and religious backgrounds, reducing prejudice and supporting peaceful living together in multi-faceted societies.

INFORMATION:

- *Address:* John-F.-Kennedy Platz 1, 10825 Berlin

- *DATE:* From 1st to 3rd December 2023

Exhibitions

❖ Lawrence Lek: NOX

NOX: Nonhuman Excellence is an expansive exhibition that invites visitors to explore a dystopian future where sentient self-driving cars are tested and trained by the fictional AI conglomerate Farsight Corporation. The exhibition forms the latest chapter in Lek's Sinofuturist cinematic universe, which explores the ethical implications of AI in an age of automation.

Through a combination of immersive storytelling and branching narratives, Lek highlights society's complex and evolving relationship with non-human entities. Visitors are led through different scenes from this fictional universe, accompanied by an evolving soundscape of ambient music and voiceover fragments from the cars and their AI therapy chatbot.

The exhibition raises questions about the psychological consequences of a future populated by smart systems and intelligent nonhumans. It also explores the concept of "NOX," a corporate psychological program created to treat undesirable behavior in automated vehicles. Some self-driving cars question their designated role in society, while others resist their future obsolescence or simply want to drive.

INFORMATION:

- *Address:* Kurfürstendamm 21-23, 10719 Berlin-Charlottenburg

- *DATE:* From 27th October to 14th January 2024

❖ Dalí Surreal

Dali's paintings are enlarged and projected onto the walls of presentation rooms, using state-of-the-art technology to bring them to life. This symbiosis of art and technology carries Dali's genius into a new age, making his poetic and fantastic universe unforgettable. Visitors can immerse themselves in Dali's art and experience his open, ambitious, provocative, and scientific mindset through larger-than-life projections of his paintings. The intriguing and extraordinary works of Surrealism's chief exponent are highlighted here!

INFORMATION:

- *Address:* *Ziegrastraße 1, 12057 Berlin-Neukölln*

- *Location: Neukölln Speicher*

- *DATE:* From 7th November to 4th February 2024

❖ Mary Ellen Mark: Encounters

Mary Ellen Mark's photography explores the full range of human experience, from intimate portraits of people on the margins of society to reportage on social challenges and moments of hope. Her work is perceptive and insightful, capturing the highs and lows of life with a humanistic, intimate, and thematic approach.

- *Address:* Hardenbergstraße 22, 10623 BerlinSeptember

- *Location:* C/O Berlin

- _DATE:_ From 16th to 18th January 2024

- _Opening Hours:_ Daily (11 am to 8 pm)

- _Admission:_ €12, reduced fee (€6)

Christmas concerts in Berlin

❖ Berlin Philharmonic Orchestra Christmas Concert

- The Berlin Philharmonic Orchestra, renowned for its world-class performances, hosts an annual Christmas concert at the Berlin Philharmonie. This prestigious event features a program of traditional carols, classical compositions, and festive favorites.

❖ Konzerthaus Berlin Christmas Concert

- The Konzerthaus Berlin, another prominent concert hall in Berlin, hosts a delightful Christmas concert featuring renowned soloists and ensembles. The program often includes a mix of traditional and contemporary holiday music, creating a captivating and festive experience.

❖ Rundfunkchor Berlin Christmas Concert

The Rundfunkchor Berlin, a renowned choir known for its exquisite vocal performances, hosts a captivating Christmas concert at the Berliner Dom, the iconic cathedral in Berlin. The program features traditional carols, sacred choral works, and festive arrangements.

❖ Komische Oper Berlin Christmas Concert

Komische Oper Berlin, a renowned opera house known for its lighthearted productions, hosts a cheerful Christmas concert at the Komische Oper Berlin. The program often features a mix of opera excerpts, popular holiday songs, and comedic elements.

❖ WeihnachtsOratorium Berlin

The WeihnachtsOratorium Berlin, a renowned choir and orchestra, presents a series of Christmas concerts throughout the season, featuring Johann Sebastian Bach's iconic Weihnachtsoratorium (Christmas Oratorio).

❖ Festive Organ Concerts

Various churches in Berlin host festive organ concerts during the Christmas season. These concerts offer a serene and contemplative atmosphere, featuring traditional carols, organ arrangements, and classical masterpieces.

❖ Christmas Jazz Concerts

Berlin's vibrant jazz scene offers a unique twist on the traditional Christmas concert. Jazz clubs and concert halls host performances featuring jazz arrangements of holiday classics and original compositions inspired by the season.

❖ Christmas Eve at Berlin Cathedral

Berlin Cathedral hosts a special Christmas Eve service and concert, creating a peaceful and reflective atmosphere for this significant evening.

❖ Christmas Gospel Concerts

Berlin features several gospel choirs that perform uplifting Christmas gospel concerts. These concerts infuse a joyful and soulful spirit into the holiday season.

CHAPTER 5: FOODS AND DRINKS AT BERLIN CHRISTMAS MARKETS

Traditional Cuisines At The Berlin Christmas Markets

As you wander through the Berlin Christmas markets, you'll find yourself surrounded by delicious smells. Here are a few of the Traditional Cuisines you can try:

1. Glühwein (Mulled Wine): Warm up with a steaming cup of Glühwein, which is mulled red wine flavored with spices like cloves and cinnamon. It's a popular Christmas drink and often served in charming, collectible mugs.

2. Schmalzkuchen: These deep-fried pastries resemble mini doughnuts and are often dusted with powdered sugar. They are small, sweet, and delightful.

3. Roasted Chestnuts (Maronen): The aroma of roasting chestnuts is a common scent at Christmas Markets. These warm, earthy treats are a comforting snack, perfect for nibbling as you explore the market.

4. Potato Pancakes (Kartoffelpuffer): These potato pancakes are crispy on the outside and tender on the inside. They're served with applesauce or a dollop of sour cream. Perfect for a savory bite.

5. Bratwurst (Sausage): German

sausages are a staple at Christmas Markets. Savor a Bratwurst, a grilled pork or veal sausage, typically served in a crusty roll with mustard or ketchup. The Nürnberger Rostbratwurst is a popular variety.

6. Lebkuchen (Gingerbread): These

gingerbread cookies are a beloved holiday treat. They come in various shapes and sizes, often elaborately decorated with icing and sugar. Look for the heart-shaped ones, known as "Herzen."

7. Stollen (Fruit Bread): Stollen is a

dense, fruit-filled Christmas bread that's a staple during the holiday season. It's packed with candied fruits, nuts, and spices, and often dusted with powdered sugar. A slice is a delightful dessert or snack.

8. Wurstsalat: This is a German sausage salad, made with slices of various sausages, onions, and a tangy vinegar-based dressing. It's a savory and satisfying dish.

9. Feuerzangenbowle: These crescent-shaped cookies boast a delightful hazelnut flavor, often adorned with a luscious chocolate glaze, adding a touch of luxury to your market visit.

10. Schweinshaxe: If you're craving something hearty, try Schweinshaxe, which is a roasted ham hock. It's a substantial meal, typically served with sauerkraut and potatoes.

11. Pretzels: These large, savory pretzels with a sprinkle of salt are a favorite snack in Austria. They're delicious on their own or enjoyed with a side of mustard or ketchup.

12. Raclette: Some Christmas Markets offer Raclette, a Swiss cheese dish. Melted cheese is scraped onto potatoes, pickles, and onions. It's a warm and cheesy delight.

13. Kinderpunsch: This non-alcoholic alternative is perfect for children and designated drivers. It's a warm, spiced fruit punch with similar spices as Glühwein.

14. Hot Chocolate: Enjoy a steaming cup of rich and creamy hot chocolate, often topped with whipped cream and chocolate shavings. Some stalls offer variations like white hot chocolate or Nutella hot chocolate.

15. Non-Alcoholic Beverages: If you're not into alcoholic drinks, many stalls offer a variety of non-alcoholic options like fruit punches, spiced teas, and hot apple cider.

International Cuisines At The Berlin Christmas Markets

1. Chimney Cake (Trdelník): Hailing from Eastern Europe, particularly the Czech Republic and Hungary, these sweet, spiral-shaped pastries are roasted over an open flame and rolled in sugar, cinnamon, and nuts. You'll find them at various Christmas Markets, offering a delightful mix of textures and flavors.

2. Döner Kebab: A popular street food in Berlin, Döner Kebab is a Turkish-inspired treat. Enjoy succulent slices of seasoned meat served in a flatbread or pita, with fresh vegetables, yogurt sauce, and various condiments.

3. Italian Pasta: Some Christmas Markets, like the one at Gendarmenmarkt, offer Italian pasta dishes such as fresh gnocchi, ravioli, and more. It's a taste of Italy right in the heart of Berlin.

4. Greek Gyros: Savor the Mediterranean flavors of Greek gyros. These seasoned and roasted meat slices are typically served on pita bread with fresh vegetables and tzatziki sauce.

5. Spanish Churros: Indulge in the warm and sugary delights of Spanish churros. These fried dough pastries are often served with a rich chocolate dipping sauce.

6. Asian Dumplings: Some Christmas Markets offer a taste of Asia with steaming hot dumplings, often filled with a variety of ingredients like pork, shrimp, or vegetables. They're served with a tasty dipping sauce.

7. Crepe Suzette: These thin French pancakes are often served with an assortment of fillings such as Nutella, strawberries, or whipped cream, offering a taste of France at the markets.

8. British Fish and Chips: At select Christmas Markets, you can relish the crispy delight of British-style fish and chips. Enjoy deep-fried fish fillets and chunky fries with a side of tartar sauce.

9. Indian Samosas: Explore the spices of India with samosas, crispy pastry pockets filled with spiced potatoes and other ingredients. They're often served with chutney.

10. Japanese Takoyaki: At certain markets, you may find these Japanese octopus-filled snack balls, takoyaki. They're cooked in a special iron griddle and served with various toppings.

Vegetarian and Vegan Christmas Market Food Options

1. Potato Dishes: Look for stalls offering Bratkartoffeln, which are pan-fried potatoes with various seasonings and toppings. They are often vegetarian and can be vegan if you ask for no butter.

2. Veggie Bratwurst: Many Christmas Markets offer vegetarian or vegan bratwurst sausages made from plant-based ingredients.

They are seasoned to perfection and served with delicious condiments.

3. Falafel: Falafel stalls are a common sight at Berlin's Christmas Markets. These deep-fried balls or patties made from ground chickpeas or fava beans are typically served on pita bread or as a platter with various toppings.

4. Roasted Chestnuts: Roasted chestnuts are a traditional Christmas treat. They are naturally vegan and can be found at various stalls. They're a warm and delicious snack.

5. Vegetable Skewers: Some stalls offer grilled vegetable skewers, perfect for a savory and healthy option. These skewers may be marinated and seasoned for extra flavor.

6. Spätzle: Spätzle is a type of soft egg noodle commonly found at the markets. Some vendors may offer vegan versions, so be sure to ask.

7. Vegan Soups: Some stalls may offer hearty vegan soups like potato soup or lentil soup, perfect for warming up on a cold day.

8. Fresh Fruit Cups: You'll find stalls selling fresh fruit cups with a variety of seasonal fruits. It's a healthy and refreshing option.

9. Nuts and Dried Fruits: Stalls with a selection of nuts and dried fruits can be a great place to grab a quick, nutritious snack.

10. Kumpir: Kumpir is a Turkish baked potato dish that's customizable with various vegan toppings like olives, corn, and veggies.

.

CHAPTER 6: SHOPPING AT BERLIN CHRISTMAS MARKETS

What Can You Buy At The Christmas Markets In Berlin?

1. Handcrafted Ornaments: Christmas Markets in Berlin are known for their beautifully handcrafted ornaments. You can find delicate glass baubles, wooden decorations, and intricately designed ornaments to adorn your Christmas tree.

2. Christmas Decorations: You can find a wide variety of Christmas decorations at the Berlin Christmas markets, including ornaments, garlands, and tree toppers.

3. Gifts and Souvenirs: Looking for something special? Browse through stalls offering a variety of gifts, from jewelry and clothing to candles and scented soaps. You're sure to find one-of-a-kind presents.

4. Incense Smokers (Räuchermännchen): These charming figures, often shaped like woodcutters, bakers, or miners, are a classic German Christmas decoration. They're designed to hold incense cones, creating a fragrant holiday ambiance.

5. Local and International Foods: Savor traditional German foods like Bratwurst, sauerkraut, and potato pancakes. You can also explore international cuisine at certain markets, with offerings ranging from Greek gyros to Italian pasta.

6. Mulled Wine Mugs: Many Christmas Markets have their collectible mugs for Glühwein (mulled wine) and other beverages. These make for great souvenirs.

7. Art and Crafts: Talented artisans showcase their work at the markets, offering everything from paintings and sculptures to upcycled accessories. These artistic treasures are a delight for art enthusiasts.

8. Textiles and Apparel: You can find cozy winter clothing, scarves, and mittens at the

markets to keep warm during your visit and bring home as functional keepsakes.

9. Gourmet Treats: Sample and purchase delectable holiday treats such as marzipan, gingerbread (Lebkuchen), and artisanal chocolates. You can also take home some of the famous German Stollen fruitcakes.

11. Candles and Candleholders: Decorative candles and candle holders are popular items at the markets. These can add a warm and cozy atmosphere to your home during the holiday season.

12. Unique Souvenirs: Take home a piece of Berlin's culture with unique souvenirs

such as Berlin-themed trinkets, postcards, and more.

13. Christmas Gifts: Find the perfect Christmas gifts for friends and family, from personalized items to quirky and one-of-a-kind presents.

14. Toys and Games: The markets feature an array of traditional and contemporary toys, puzzles, and games for children and the young at heart.

15. Handmade Crafts: Browse stalls selling handcrafted gifts like knitted scarves, mittens, and other textiles, as well as pottery, jewelry, and leather goods made by local artisans.

16. Festive Apparel: Get into the holiday spirit by purchasing festive apparel like Christmas sweaters, hats, and scarves. You can even find clothing with unique German designs.

Tips For Shopping At Berlin Christmas markets

1. Cash is King: Many stalls at Christmas Markets prefer cash payments. While some larger stalls may accept cards, it's a good idea to carry some cash with you. ATMs are often available at or near the markets, but they might charge fees.

2. Bring Your Bag: Consider bringing your reusable shopping bag. It's both environmentally friendly and useful for carrying your items.

3. Sample Before Buying: Many stalls offer free samples of their products. Don't hesitate to taste the local treats and try out handmade goods before making a purchase.

4. Early Bird Gets the Worm: If you want to avoid crowds, consider visiting the markets early in the day when they open. You'll have a more peaceful shopping experience.

5. Take Your Time: Don't rush through the markets. Take your time to explore each

stall, enjoy the festive atmosphere, and find unique gifts.

6. Try Local Foods: Savor the local foods and drinks offered at the markets. Don't miss out on trying traditional treats like Bratwurst, Glühwein (mulled wine), Stollen, and roasted chestnuts.

7. Collectible Mugs: When you order Glühwein or other drinks at the markets, you'll often receive a collectible mug with a deposit. You can return the mug for your deposit or keep it as a souvenir.

8. Be Mindful of Allergies: If you have food allergies or specific dietary requirements,

ask the vendors about the ingredients used in their products to ensure they're safe for you.

9. Keep an Eye on Your Belongings: Like in any crowded place, it's essential to keep an eye on your belongings to ensure a safe and enjoyable shopping experience.

10. Check Opening Hours: Confirm the opening and closing times of the markets you plan to visit, as they can vary between different markets.

11. Plan Your Route: Plan your shopping route by marking the stalls or markets you want

to visit on a map or navigation app. It can help you navigate the markets more efficiently.

12. Bring a Shopping List: If you have specific gifts in mind, make a shopping list to help you stay focused and not forget any important items.

CHAPTER 7: FAMILY FUN AT BERLIN CHRISTMAS MARKETS

Christmas Market Activities for Kids of All Ages

1. Visit Santa Claus: Many Christmas Markets have Santa Claus (or "Weihnachtsmann" in German) in attendance. Kids can meet Santa, take photos, and share their wish lists.

2. Carousel Rides: Carousels adorned with beautiful lights and festive decorations are a hit with kids. Let them enjoy a ride on one of these classic attractions.

3. Petting Zoos: Several markets feature small petting zoos with friendly animals like goats, sheep, and ponies. Kids can interact with the animals and as well feed them.

4. Puppet Shows: Puppet theaters and shows are a common sight at many Christmas Markets. Kids of all ages can enjoy the lively performances.

5. Storytelling: Look for stalls or areas where storytellers captivate young audiences with enchanting tales and holiday stories.

6. Fairground Games: Try your hand at traditional fairground games like ring toss or balloon darts. Prizes and small gifts are often awarded to winners.

7. Craft Workshops: Some markets host craft workshops where kids can create ornaments, candles, and other holiday-themed crafts.

8. Ice Skating: Some Christmas Markets have ice skating rinks. Skating is a classic winter activity that kids of all ages can enjoy.

9. Kid-Friendly Food: Look for kid-friendly food options like crepes, waffles, cotton candy, and chocolate-covered fruit.

10. Light Displays: Admire the enchanting light displays and illuminated decorations that are sure to capture kids' imaginations.

11. Kids' Shopping: Let kids experience the joy of shopping by giving them a small budget to choose their holiday gifts or ornaments.

12. Miniature Trains: Miniature train displays are a hit with kids. These displays often feature intricate landscapes and moving trains.

Tips for Visiting Berlin Christmas Markets with Kids

1. Plan Your Visit: Check the dates and locations of Berlin's Christmas Markets. Decide which ones to visit and plan your itinerary.

2. Dress for the Weather: Berlin can be quite cold during the winter, so dress your kids warmly. Layering is key to staying comfortable in changing temperatures.

3. Stay Comfortable: Wear comfortable shoes for walking and exploring the markets. If you have a stroller for young children, it can be helpful for tired legs.

4. Set Expectations: Talk to your kids about what to expect at the Christmas Markets. Explain the festive atmosphere, food, and the possibility of meeting Santa Claus or other characters.

5. Keep an Eye on Kids: The markets can be crowded, so always keep an eye on your children. Teach them to look for designated meeting points in case they get separated.

6. Collect Souvenirs: Let your children pick out a small souvenir or ornament to remember the trip. This makes the experience more special for them.

7. Stay Hydrated: Don't forget to drink water throughout the day. Markets can be deceptively dehydrating, especially in cold weather.

8. Rest Breaks: Take breaks when needed. Some markets have seating areas where you can warm up, enjoy a snack, and rest for a bit.

9. Safety First: Teach your children to be cautious and avoid touching open flames or hot surfaces used for cooking. Safety is essential.

10. Stay Together: It's easy for kids to get lost in the crowd. Consider using child harnesses or bracelets with contact information to stay connected.

CHAPTER 8

Useful German Phrases for Berlin Christmas Markets

➢ **Guten Tag!** — Good day!

➢ **Guten Abend!** — Good evening

➢ **"Frohe Weihnachten"** — (Merry Christmas)

➢ **"Alles Gute im neuen Jahr" or "Guten Rutsch"** — (Happy New Year)

➢ **Grüß Gott!** — Hello!

➢ **Auf Wiedersehen!** — Goodbye

➢ **Entschuldigung, bitte.** — Excuse me, please

➢ **Dankeschön.** — Thank you

➢ **Können Sie mir helfen?** — Can you help me?

➢ **Einen schönen Tag noch!** — Have a nice day!

➢ **Viel Spaß!** — Have fun

➢ **Ich suche** … I'm looking for…

➢ **Wo ist ... zu finden?** — Where can…. Be found?

➢ **Können Sie mir bitte eine Karte zeigen?** — Can you please show me a map?

➢ **Wo ist bitte der nächste Weihnachtsmarkt?** — Where is the nearest Christmas market please?

➢ **Ich möchte….** I would like…

➢ **Wie viel kostet das?** — How much is it?

➢ **Ich möchte gerne zahlen.** — I would like to pay

➢ **Nehmen Sie Bargeld oder Kreditkarten?** — Do you take cash or credit cards?

- ➢ **"Ein Glühwein, bitte"** — A mulled wine, please

- ➢ **Ich hätte gerne eine Bratwurst, bitte.** — I would like a bratwurst, please.

- ➢ **"Das ist wunderschön!"** — That is beautiful

- ➢ **"Wo ist die nächste Toilette?"** — Where is the nearest restroom?

- ➢ **"Schmeckt das gut?"** — Does it taste good??

- ➢ **Kann ich das bitte probieren?** — Can I try this, please?

- ➢ **Können Sie das bitte für mich einpacken?** — Can you please wrap this up for me?

- ➢ **"Das ist ein schönes Geschenk"** — This is a nice gift

CONCLUSION

And so, my fellow holiday enthusiast, we've come to the wonderful end of our festive journey through Berlin's Christmas Markets. It's been a pleasure being your guide through this magical season.

As we close the pages of this guidebook, I want to express my heartfelt gratitude to you for choosing to explore Berlin's yuletide charm with us. Your curiosity and spirit have added an extra dash of magic to our adventure.

You and I have wandered the dazzling stalls, indulged in the delicious treats, and shared a moment of wonder beneath the twinkling lights. It's been a delightful journey, hasn't it?

Now, as you embark on your holiday adventures in Berlin, may your days be filled with laughter, your heart with joy, and your memories be as warm as a cup of mulled wine on a cold winter evening.

From the bottom of my heart, I wish you the merriest of Christmases and a holiday season filled with love, laughter, and the kind of enchantment that only Berlin's Christmas Markets can provide. ***Merry Christmas and Happy Holidays, my friend!*** 🎄🔔✨

BONUS SECTION

Christmas Shopping Planner

THIS CHRISTMAS
SHOPPING PLANNER

Belongs to:

....

....

My Christmas
SHOPPING PLANNER

DATE: _____

THINGS TO BUY	BUDGET	ACTUAL PRICE

My Christmas
SHOPPING PLANNER

DATE: _____

THINGS TO BUY	BUDGET	ACTUAL PRICE

My Christmas
SHOPPING PLANNER

DATE: _____

THINGS TO BUY	BUDGET	ACTUAL PRICE

My Christmas
SHOPPING PLANNER

DATE: _____

THINGS TO BUY	BUDGET	ACTUAL PRICE

My Christmas
SHOPPING PLANNER

DATE: —————————

THINGS TO BUY	BUDGET	ACTUAL PRICE

My Christmas
SHOPPING PLANNER

DATE: _____

THINGS TO BUY	BUDGET	ACTUAL PRICE

My Christmas
SHOPPING PLANNER

DATE: _____

THINGS TO BUY	BUDGET	ACTUAL PRICE

167

My Christmas
SHOPPING PLANNER

DATE: _____

THINGS TO BUY	BUDGET	ACTUAL PRICE

My Christmas
SHOPPING PLANNER

DATE: _____

THINGS TO BUY	BUDGET	ACTUAL PRICE

My Christmas
SHOPPING PLANNER

DATE: _____

THINGS TO BUY	BUDGET	ACTUAL PRICE

NOTE:

NOTE:

NOTE:

NOTE:

Printed in Great Britain
by Amazon

34219694R00097